MW01048967

KARMA,
DHARMA,
PUDDING & PIE

KARMA, DHARMA, PUDDING & PIE

Philip Appleman

ILLUSTRATIONS BY
ARNOLD ROTH

FOREWORD BY X. J. KENNEDY

The Quantuck Lane Press
New York

Karma, Dharma, Pudding & Pie
Philip Appleman

Copyright © 2009 by Philip Appleman
Foreword copyright © 2009 by X. J. Kennedy
Illustrations copyright © 2009 by Arnold Roth

Book design and composition by Laura Lindgren
The text of this book is composed in Wessex.

Library of Congress Cataloging-in-Publication Data
Appleman, Philip, 1926–
  Karma, dharma, pudding & pie / Philip Appleman ; illustrations
by Arnold Roth ; foreword by X. J. Kennedy. — 1st ed.
    p.   cm.
  ISBN 978-1-59372-036-0
 I. Roth, Arnold, 1929– II. Title. III. Title: Karma, dharma,
pudding and pie.
  PS3551.P6K37 2009
  811'.54—dc22   2008047315

The Quantuck Lane Press | New York
www.quantucklanepress.com

Distributed by
W. W. Norton & Company
500 Fifth Avenue
New York, NY 10110
www.wwnorton.com

1 2 3 4 5 6 7 8 9 0

ALSO BY PHILIP APPLEMAN

POETRY
New and Selected Poems, 1956–1996 (University of Arkansas Press, 1996)
Let There Be Light (HarperCollins, 1991)
Darwin's Bestiary (Echo Press, 1986)
Darwin's Ark (Indiana University Press, 1984)
Open Doorways (W. W. Norton, 1976)
Summer Love and Surf (Vanderbilt University Press, 1968)
Kites on a Windy Day (Byron Press, England, 1967)

FICTION
Apes and Angels (G. P. Putnam's Sons, 1989)
Shame the Devil (Crown Publishers, 1981)
In the Twelfth Year of the War (G. P. Putnam's Sons, 1970)

NONFICTION
The Silent Explosion (Beacon Press, 1965)

EDITED WORKS
Darwin (W. W. Norton, 1970; 2001)
Malthus on Population (W. W. Norton, 1976; 2004)
The Origin of Species (W. W. Norton, 1975; 2002)
1859: Entering an Age of Crisis (Indiana University Press, 1959)
Victorian Studies (founding coeditor, 1957–1963)

for Margie, who finds the fun in life

If a man insisted always on being serious, and never allowed himself a bit of fun and relaxation, he would go mad.
—Herodotus

One wants to keep one's hand in, you know, in every type of poem, serious and frivolous and proper and improper.
—T. S. Eliot

CONTENTS

ACKNOWLEDGMENTS

Grateful acknowledgment is made to the following publications, in which the poems in this book first appeared, some in slightly different versions.

College English: "Petals on a Wet, Black Bough"

Confrontation: "Parable of the Talents"

Falmouth Review: "Prairie Dogs"

Free Inquiry: "Five Easy Prayers for Pagans"

Freethought Today: "Parable of the Perfidious Proverbs," "Parable of the One-Track Mind," "Intelligent? Design?" "On the Seventh Day," "The Doctor-Killer Reads His Bible," "A Simple Explanation for Everything," "Reverend Euphemism Admonishes the Skeptics," "Reading the Headlines"

The Humanist: "Not for Love"

Light: "Said," "The End of the World," "Horoscope," "Why Lamarck Became Extinct," "God's Grandeur," "That Time of Year," "Maxims for Diverse Occasions," "Cramming for Finals," "Arise, Take Up Thy Bed, and Walk," "Nightingales and Roses," "S*x after S*xty"

Long Island Quarterly: "The Parliament of Man, the Federation of the World"

New York Times: "Saturday, in Color"

Poetry: "Arts & Sciences"

FOREWORD

E. B. White once maintained that a writer of comic verse works just as hard as a serious poet. No doubt Philip Appleman toiled hard in writing *Karma, Dharma, Pudding & Pie*, but such is his skill that you don't even notice any perspiration. Take the first poem of the book, "Five Easy Prayers for Pagans," a blooming masterpiece whose rollicking measures roll off the page with seeming ease. Moreover, Appleman is a master of the sonnet, the terse rhymed epigram, and even that fiendishly ingenious form the double dactyl (see "Said"). To watch him sling words is to be richly regaled.

No mere prosodist, he likes to say something. Several of the poems wax skeptical about established beliefs and observances, and smack of secular freethinking. Since I'm a faithful ex-Catholic, they make my hackles rise. Theology, says Appleman, is the sport of the upper classes; true believers belong in the loony bin. He throws cold water on the custom of piously killing people whose religion you don't share and high-handedly rewrites Scripture. I reckon that the pope would get off his throne and excommunicate Appleman in a jiffy, if only Appleman were a Catholic, but he isn't, so maybe this point is moot. In any case, he also gives a few deserving Jews and Muslims, fundamentalists, and Presbyterians a friendly going-over with the brass knucks. He deals the acid around most equitably.

Neither does it hurt that, as you can see, this book has terrific drawings by the immortal Arnold Roth of *New Yorker*, *Punch*, and *Playboy* celebrity. *Karma, Dharma, Pudding & Pie* must be the best-illustrated book since the monks of Iona drudged with pen and gold leaf illuminating the Book of Kells. But let me not belabor the obvious.

Anyhow, Philip Appleman would qualify for the label Renaissance man if only he could sculpt, play the ukulele, and design airplanes. Not that his accomplishments aren't plenty. Poet, novelist, scholar, editor, and social critic, he is also (believe it or not) a widely known expert on Darwin, Malthus, and the origin of species.

Well, now Appleman can add "wit" to his designations, although usually for a poet to be branded a wit doesn't raise his stock any. In America today, light verse is consigned to the doghouse of literature. Maybe Ogden Nash and Dorothy Parker are still respected by the discerning. But a really good poet, the theory runs, ought to be as sober as a hanging judge, preoccupied with important abstractions like the Parliament of Man and excess gastric acidity. (Actually, Appleman does give the Parliament of Man a passing nod, but he doesn't take it too seriously.) The prevalence of such notions is unfortunate. It could discourage us from reading funny verse and having a better time.

Still, I confidently predict that you'll have a fine time reading Philip Appleman's brilliant, hilarious, technically dazzling poetic flights, no doubt about it. Indeed, let me make you a money-back guarantee. If you don't like the book, just send your copy to me care of this publisher by registered mail together with your sales slip, a notarized letter stating reasons for your discontent, and twenty-five dollars in cash for postage and handling, and I'll send you half of your money back. No questions asked. Have a good day.

X. J. Kennedy

I.

THIS IS
THE WAY
THE WORLD
GOES 'ROUND

FIVE EASY PRAYERS FOR PAGANS

1

O Karma, Dharma, pudding & pie,
gimme a break before I die:
grant me wisdom, will, & wit,
purity, probity, pluck, & grit.
Trustworthy, helpful, friendly, kind,
gimme great abs and a steel-trap mind.
And forgive, Ye Gods, some humble advice—
these little blessings would suffice
to beget an earthly paradise:
make the bad people good
and the good people nice,
and before our world goes over the brink,
teach the believers how to think.

2

O Venus, Cupid, Aphrodite,
teach us Thy horsepower lingam, Thy firecracker yoni.
Show us Thy hundreds of sacred & tingling positions,
each orifice panting for every groping tumescence.
O lead us into the back rooms of silky temptation
and deliver us over to midnights of trembling desire.
But before all the nectar & honey leak out of this planet,
give us our passion in marble, commitment in granite.

3

O Shiva, relentless Spirit of Outrage:
in this vale of tearful True Believers,
teach us to repeat again and again:
No, your Reverences, we will not serve
your Gross National Voodoo, your Church
Militant—we will not flatter the double faces
of those who pray in the Temple of
Incendiary Salvation.
Gentle Preserver, preserve the pure irreverence
of our stubborn minds.
Target the priests, Implacable Destroyer—
and hire a lawyer.

4

O Mammon, Thou who art daily dissed
by everyone, yet boast more true disciples
than all other gods together,
Thou whose eerie sheen
gleameth from Corporate Headquarters
and Vatican Treasury alike, Thou
whose glittering eye impales us
in the X-ray vision of plastic surgeons,
the golden leer of televangelists,
the star-spangled gloat of politicos—
O Mammon, come down to us in the form
of Treasuries, Annuities, & High-Grade Bonds,
yield unto us those Benedict Arnold Funds,
those Quicksand Convertible Securities, even the wet
Judas Kiss of Futures Contracts—for
unto the least of these Thy supplicants
art Thou welcome in all Thy many forms. But
when Thou comest to say we're finally in the gentry—
use the service entry.

5

O flaky Goddess of Fortune, we beseech Thee:
in the random thrust of Thy fluky favor, vector
the luminous lasers of Thy shifty eyes
down upon these, Thy needy & oh-so-deserving
petitioners. Bend down to us the sexy
curve of Thine indifferent ear, and hear
our passionate invocation: let Thy lovely,
lying lips murmur to us the news
of all our true-false guesses A-OK,
our firm & final offers come up rainbows,
our hangnails & hang-ups & hangovers suddenly zapped,
and then, O Goddess, give us your slippery word
that the faithless Lady Luck will hang around
in our faithful love, friendships less fickle than youth,
and a steady view of our world in its barefoot truth.

ARTS & SCIENCES

Everyone carries around in the back of his mind the wreck of a thing he calls his education.

—Stephen Leacock

SOLID GEOMETRY
Here's a nice thought we can save:
The luckiest thing about sex
Is: you happen to be so concave
In the very same place I'm convex.

BOTANY
Your thighs always blossomed like orchids,
You had rose hips when we danced,
But the question that always baffled me was:
How *can* I get into those plants?

ECONOMICS
Diversification's a virtue,
And as one of its multiple facets,
When we're merging, it really won't hurt you
To share your disposable assets.

GEOGRAPHY
Russian you would be deplorable,
But your Lapland is simply Andorrable
So my Hungary fantasy understands
Why I can't keep my hands off your Netherlands.

LIT SURVEY

Alexander composed like the Pope,
Swift was of course never tardy,
And my Longfellow's Wildest hope
Is to find you right next to my Hardy.

PHYSICS

If E is how eager I am for you,
And m is your marvelous body,
And c means the caring I plan for you,
Then E = Magna Cum Laude.

MUSIC APPRECIATION

You're my favorite tune, my symphony,
So please do me this favor:
Don't ever change, not even a hemi-
Demi-semiquaver.

ART APPRECIATION

King Arthur, betrayed by Sir Lancelot,
Blamed the poets who'd praised him, and spake:
"That knight's nights are in the Queen's pantsalot,
So from now on your art's for *Art's* sake."

ABSTRACT EXPRESSIONISM

I couldn't do Goyas or Grecos,
And my Rembrandts had zero panache,
But after I junked all my brushes,
My canvases made quite a splash.

PHILOSOPHY

1. BLAISE PASCAL
Pascal, reflecting tearfully
On our wars for the Holy Pigeon,
Said, "Alas, we do evil most cheerfully
When we do it for religion."

2. RENÉ DESCARTES
The unruly dactyls and anapests
Were thumping their wild dithyrambic
When Descartes with a scowl very sternly stressed:
"I think, therefore iambic!"

3. THOMAS HOBBES
Better at thinking than loving,
He deserved his wife's retort:
On their wedding night, she told him, "Tom,
That was nasty, brutish—*and short!*"

THE PARLIAMENT OF MAN,
THE FEDERATION OF THE WORLD

The Labrador is hounding a French poodle,
The Persian kitten nipped the neighbor's Scottie,
The Siamese Fighting Fish ate the Peruvian
Longfin, and is gulping at a guppy.

Japanese beetles vandalize the Swiss chard,
Dutch elm disease has blighted Kalamazoo,
Kansas kids are catching German measles,
And Maine reports a plague of Asian flu.

So goes the nation—and, in fact, the world:
Our skin is our frontier, our life's a border.
World Order is a dream; we're making do
With what we've got—the same old Pecking Order.

THE END OF THE WORLD

It could all go up in a flash, of course:
a comet collision, a sneaky nuke,
or a gutting from some galactic god
we've never even heard of. But
those are long shots, after all,
doomsday daydreams. Ten to one
there'll be no Roman candles at all,
only
some slick guy in a three-piece suit
staring out of the big screen, eyes
gazing into yours, sincere as a stockbroker,
his voice like melting chocolate
telling you God is on our side,
but we need those big battalions;
saying conglomerates are good for you,
treasure's tidbits trickling down;
telling you guns don't kill people, and
the pregnant power of prayer
will fix your furry fungus.
And
the very last words you'll hear
before the final blackout will be
"Trust me."

MAXIMS FOR DIVERSE OCCASIONS

Bedeviled by malaise and moral cancers,
Everyone is hot for easy answers:
What this country needs, before cremation,
Is two cents' worth of Instant Meditation.
So, little rhymes, go spread your moral jargon:
Wisdom's rare, but preaching is a bargain.

* * *

Education
Education is whatever you cannot forget:
    Answers are easy, questions are always a threat.
    Ignorance hurts, in surgeons and taxi drivers.
    When truths drop dead, paradox whips the survivors.

Religion
Creeds are easier to learn than unlearn:
    Fanatics end with sainthood or with sunburn.
    Theology's the sport of the upper classes.
    Masses are the opiate of the masses.

Art
Art is what's left when you burn away the fact:
    A poem, like prayer, is an unnatural act.
    Brick is forever, marble is frightfully fickle.
    Without symbolism, two dimes would buy a nickel.

Style
Style is what keeps bread from being cake:
    Hamburger is the very quintessence of steak.
    Strong views, like strong eggs, need a pinch of salt.
    Mold is an accident, Roquefort is somebody's fault.

Civilization
Civilizations depend on garbage men:
    Progress can turn a lake into a fen.
    To own a tree is shameless impudence.
    Good fences always make good arguments.

* * *

Platitudes come easy, silence hard.
Advice is always simple to discard.
So go, little rhymes, but don't be in a hurry:
When chaos whispers, men say, "What, *me* worry?"
Most prefer hot cures to cool prevention.
Wisdom shrugs when no one pays attention.

II.

TELLING
IT
SLANT

SATURDAY, IN COLOR

Kids in pink pajamas sit enraptured
As wily mice outwit the wicked cat
And brainy bears elude their human captors
And scrappy rabbits hit back, tit for tat.
The moral, in the land of Krispie Krunchies,
Is worms can turn, and bullies get the worst,
That little lads can land the lucky punches—
In short, that nice guys always finish first.

But after lunch their Dad kicks off his Loafers,
Tunes in to his reality, and swears
As Tigers gobble up the gallant Gophers
And Purple Panthers maul the Golden Bears.
Real heads are busted with Dad's benediction,
Hard knocks are what he recommends for schools.
And yet his fight is far less fact than fiction:
Those busted heads are busted by the rules.

In prime time Mom refuses to despair if
Some grimmer truth comes at her with a jolt:
If Robin Hood is gunned down by the sheriff,
The Noble Savage slaughtered by the Colt,
If war erupts again in crimson mayhem
And God is out there somewhere, loading dice—
For slowly   surely   Saturday's next A.M.
Is rolling 'round again, with all those mice.

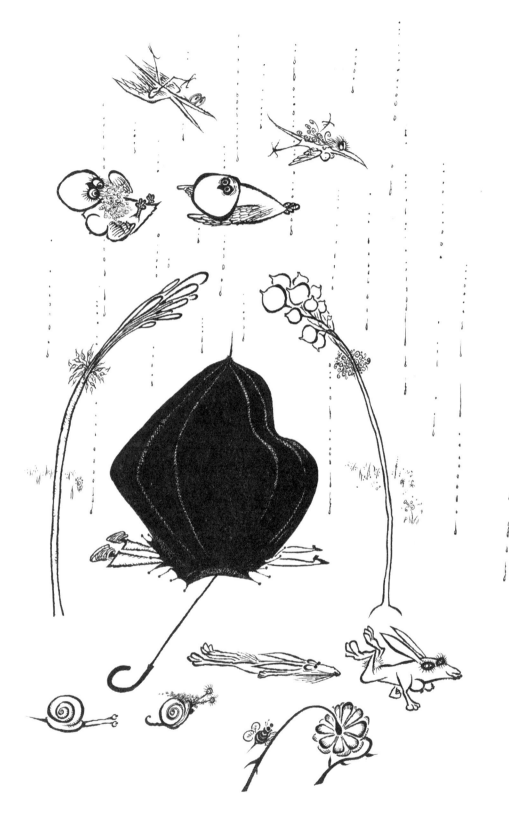

THAT TIME OF YEAR

So April's here, with all these soggy showers,
Making us almost long for March again,
As every twiglet makes a play for flowers
And every hack for miles picks up a pen,
Girls all playing hankypank, not soccer,
The smell of oozing sap all over town,
Teenage boys completely off their rocker,
And rutting rabbits diddling farmer Brown.

We're in for it now, nothing to be done:
Loving's what we wanted, what we got.
At least we're going to have a little fun—
With any luck, we're going to have a lot.
Thirty days hath April: seize the day!
Don't trust to luck for darling buds in May.

SAID

Catch-as-can Appleman:
"Marjorie Haberkorn,
you with the daringly
dingdongy name,
somehow your sonorous
sesquipedalian
cognomenation just
sets me aflame—

syllables tinkling and
jingling like glockenspiels
tickle my ventricles
charmingly—but
dactyls are dangerous,
hyperconcupiscent,
polylibidinous—
we'd better put

both of our names in an
epithalamion:
think of the singular
medley you'd make—
Marjorie Haberkorn
Appleman couldn't be
taken for anyone
else by mistake."

CRAMMING FOR FINALS

End of term, will a six-pack do us
while we speed-read Upton Sinclair Lewis?
So far behind, can we possibly ever
catch up on E. A. Robinson Jeffers?
Who said it was going to be multiple choice
on the later work of O. Henry James Joyce?
What's the plot of *The Rise of Silas Marner*? Who
remembers the Swiss Family Robinson Cru-
soe? Midnight—late. One A.M.—tardy.
Was Laurence Sterne? Was Thomas Hardy?
And hey—was John Gay?
Oh, let's take a break and all get mellow,
take our chances on Henry Wordsworth Longfellow,
and maybe later give a lick and a promise
to the earlier lyrics of Bob Dylan Thomas.

PETALS ON A WET, BLACK BOUGH

At home in **St.-Germain-des-Prés**,
Grown generous on Dubonnet,
Our wit shines from this central sun
To the wilds of **Sèvres-Babylone**,
And sheds the glow of the Deux Magots
To darkest **Denfert-Rochereau**.
Still,
When the blue-eyed girl in the yellow skirt,
Swaying from waist to thigh past **Louvre** and **Halles**,
Finished her croissant, licked her hand like a cat,
And vanished up the stairs at **Château d'Eau**—
I caught a flash of sky, of purple blossoms,
Of orange tiles and fountains in the wind . . .
And now I cannot keep from wondering:
What's out at the ends of the world? At **Pyrénées**?
At **Ternes**? At **Réamur-Sébastopol**?
Can a rose be a rose be a rose around **Crimée**
As it is as it is at the Dome and the Coupole?

I shall go, some day, to the **Porte Maillot**
And watch the Bois fill up with snow.

NIGHTINGALES AND ROSES:
THE DESERT AT SHIRAZ

Come sing to me in the garden,
Of a bowl and a lute and a kiss.
Like the zephyrs that whisper in Eden,
Sing of thrushes and blushes and bliss.
Sing a tune of the blooming of jasmine,
Of stars in the far morning air,
Yearning arms in a tracery casement,
And maidens ineffably fair,
Of ambrosia and nectar and jewels,
And meadows and magic and youth,
Of ecstasy, tears, and avowals,
And towers and trumpets and truth . . .

Alas, with a crackle of crystal
The silver streams muddy to lead,
And the bulbuls and parakeets listen
To the wail of an age that is dead.

Now passion is a pimp for any preacher,
And spring is holding out for bigger tips.
The nymphs are casting leers like any lecher,
And a desert has buried our gardens and sighs
    with a blast from its hot prosy lips.

S*X AFTER S*XTY

Forget about flowers that bloom in the spring
and hillocky bulls in the swelter of summer, this
is no skittish April day, this is ripe
October, flashing its crimson and gold
over vistas of voluptuous hills;
this is the endless sea, the tempting waves
swelling to climax on the shore,
the wreath of the long-distance runner,
the ultimate marathon, flood tide
of the Ninth Symphony, Ulysses
come at last to the Happy Isles,
Paradise Regained!
You kids in your fifties, listen,
if you think it's perfect now, just hang around:
the best is yet to come.

III.

BIBLE 101

.

PARABLE OF THE TALENTS

"I should have received mine own with interest."
—Matthew 25:27

The love of money is the root,
the branch, the flower—so
why don't we ever write poems
about money?
Is it because we're just
too good for this world, counting
our delicate heartbeats out at the edge
of everyone else's reality,
our sensitive psyches never fed
by the Fed, our Tao out of sync
with the Dow, in the midst of rallies,
all of us bearish on bulls?

Or is it because they're already
writing their own poems, those canny
can-do capitalists, brokers and bankers all busily
locking in yields,
pumping new blood into partnerships,
watching the markets peak and bottom out,
sheltering windfalls, letting their profits run,
cutting their losses,
beefing up capital, funneling cash
into balanced portfolios?

Down here in the daffodils,
who's counting? Could we ever
achieve an emotional high
at a boost in the prime rate?
Or could we go broke again
and convince our down-side lovers
it was only a negative cash flow?

No poems except
in passion: the brokers keep asking,
is her smile worth three points
up front? Will the bougainvillea
turn a profit this quarter?
Are those gentle fingertips
economically viable?
And the sonnets keep whispering: Poets,
remember,
where your treasure is,
there will your songs be also.

PARABLE OF THE ONE-TRACK MIND

The Book of Jeremiah:
"Thou hast polluted the land with thy whoredoms
and with thy wickedness . . . thou hadst a
whore's forehead, thou refusedst to be ashamed."

The Book of Ezekiel:
"They committed whoredoms in Egypt; they
committed whoredoms in their youth: there . . .
they bruised the teats of their virginity."

The Book of Hosea:
"Go, take unto thee a wife of whoredoms and
children of whoredoms: for the land hath
committed great whoredom."

The Book of Isaiah:
"The Lord will visit Tyre, and she . . . shall
commit fornication with all the kingdoms of the
world."

The Book of Amos:
"Thy wife shall be an harlot in the city . . .
and thou shalt die in a polluted land."

The Book of Joel:
"They have cast lots for my people; and have
given a boy for an harlot, and sold a girl for
wine, that they might drink."

The Book of Revelation:
"I will shew unto thee the judgment of the
great whore that sitteth upon many waters:
   With whom the kings of the earth have
committed fornication, and inhabitants of the
earth have been made drunk with the wine of her
fornication . . .
   And the woman was arrayed in purple and
scarlet colour, and decked with gold and precious

stones and pearls, having a golden cup in her
hand full of abominations and filthiness of her
fornications:

And upon her forehead was a name written,
MYSTERY, BABYLON THE GREAT, THE MOTHER OF
    HARLOTS
AND ABOMINATIONS OF THE EARTH."

Exegesis #1:
"Whosoever looketh on a woman to lust after her
hath committed adultery with her already in his
heart."

Exegesis #2:
"He that goeth about as a talebearer revealeth
secrets."

PARABLE OF THE PERFIDIOUS PROVERBS

How better it is to get wisdom than gold.
    Money buys prophets and teachers, poems and art,
    So listen, if you're so rich, why aren't you smart?

He that spareth his rod hateth his son.
    That line gives you a perfect way of testing
    Your inner feelings about child molesting.

He that maketh haste to be rich shall not be innocent.
    But here at the parish we don't find it overly hard
    To accept his dirty cash or credit card.

Hope deferred maketh the heart sick.
    That's just why the good Lord made it mandatory
    To eat your heart out down in Purgatory.

Wisdom is better than rubies.
    Among the jeweled bishops and other boobies
    It's also a whole lot rarer than rubies.

He that trusteth in his own heart is a fool.
    Trusting your heart may not be awfully bright,
    But trusting Proverbs is an idiot's delight.

GOD'S GRANDEUR

"God will laugh at the trial of the innocent."

—Job, 9:23

When they hunger and thirst, and I send down a famine,
When they pray for the sun, and I drown them with rain,
And they beg me for reasons, my only reply is:
I never apologize, never explain.

When the Angel of Death is a black wind around them
And children are dying in terrible pain,
Then they burn little candles in churches, but still
I never apologize, never explain.

When the Christians kill Jews, and Jews kill the Muslims,
And Muslims kill writers they think are profane,
They clamor for peace, or for reasons, at least,
But I never apologize, never explain.

When they wail about murder and torture and rape,
When unlucky Abel complains about Cain,
And they ask me just why I had planned it like this,
I never apologize, never explain.

Of course, if they're smart, they can figure it out—
The best of all reasons is perfectly plain.
It's because I just happen to like it this way—
So I never apologize, never explain.

A SIMPLE EXPLANATION FOR EVERYTHING

When the Syrians came down like a wolf on the fold,
Ahab of Israel sharpened his sword,
And soon the Jordan was running with blood.
    Why did they kill?
    They killed for the Lord.

When Muhammad ran off to Medina, he swore
He would roar back to Mecca, this time with a horde
Of warriors thirsting for infidel gore.
    Why did they kill?
    They killed for the Lord.

When the Pope's Inquisition put thousands in chains,
Their bodies were broken and branded and gored,
And the innocent perished in spasms of pain.
    Why did they kill?
    They killed for the Lord.

When Puritans filled all New England with dread,
Hunting down women whose thoughts they abhorred,
They strung up the witches until they were dead.
    Why did they kill?
    They killed for the Lord.

Now our Born-Agains tell us God gives them the word:
Send infidels off to their blazing reward!
So far-away rivers are running with blood.
    Why are we killing?
    We kill for the Lord.

REVEREND EUPHEMISM
ADMONISHES THE SKEPTICS

You secular humanists say it's a "War
Of Religion," but that's just impertinence:
This isn't "Religious Warfare,"
It's only Sectarian Violence.

You atheists only seem interested in
Something that you can revile, hence
You babble "Religious Warfare"
When it's only Sectarian Violence.

It's true we kill thousands of heathens, because
They're infidels in the most vile sense—
But don't say "Religious Warfare"
When it's only Sectarian Violence.

READING THE HEADLINES

Lusty priests paw kids in dusty Texas.
In floral Florida, where love goes oral,
Preachers grope the organs of their organists.
Oh, why can't pious people just be moral?

In Maine a pastor snitches widows' pennies,
In court his *mea culpa* is pathetic.
Church trustees embezzle from the many.
Oh, why do pious people have no ethics?

In Brooklyn rabbis can't disguise their *Greed*,
In Georgia, *Envy* causes priests to quarrel,
In Tehran, mullahs' *Wrath* makes many bleed.
Oh, why can't pious people just be moral?

Religious people have their explanations, and
They don't *need* morals like, say, you and me,
For Protestants elect "Predestination," and
When Catholics mouth Hail Marys, they're home free.

THE DOCTOR-KILLER READS HIS BIBLE

*"The defendant's attorney argued that the killing of
those who performed abortions was 'consistent with
biblical truth.'"*

　　　　　　　　　—*New York Times*, November 1, 1994

　　　　It is written:

　　　　"The Lord God is
　　　　a consuming fire,
　　　　eye for eye,
　　　　tooth for tooth,
　　　　burning for burning;
　　　　so cast out devils,
　　　　kill ever woman
　　　　who has known a man,
　　　　stone her with stones
　　　　that she might die . . .

　　　　for it is written:

　　　　"Thou shalt not suffer
　　　　a witch to live,
　　　　beware of men
　　　　defiled of women,
　　　　destroy young and old
　　　　with the edge of the sword,
　　　　scorch them with fire
　　　　　(serpents among you,
　　　　　　bad seed)
　　　　the sword to slay,
　　　　dogs to tear,
　　　　beasts of the field
　　　　to devour and destroy,
　　　　and let the dead
　　　　bury the dead . . . "

for it is written:

"There shall be wailing
and gnashing of teeth,
famine and plague,
generations of vipers,
locusts and scorpions,
fathers shall eat
their sons, sons
shall eat their fathers,
bad seed,
strike them,
destroy them utterly,
show no mercy,
carcasses falling
like dung on the field . . .

"All these things
the Lord has spoken:
fear the Lord
and obey, for *it
is written.*"

ARISE, TAKE UP THY BED, AND WALK

—Mark, 2:9

Motel boozy-woozy you
hardly hear the jangle or
the robot voice: time /
temperature / the brassy command,
Have a Nice Day—and the old routine
revs up again: the kegel-
squeezing rush to the john /
bleary wash / dry / comb /
pants / shirt / socks /
and then,
bag crammed, jammed, and zipped,
you tug and curse, and with a piggy grunt,
roll the mattress up
and squeeze it under your arm,
scrunch through the door,
down the hall, past
the frog-eyed desk clerk,
and out to the parking lot, where
you huff and puff and stuff it all
into the trunk.
Sweating behind the wheel
as the car burps into life,
you think:
    but He made it sound so easy
    in the book.

ON THE SEVENTH DAY

He rested, and thought it over.
What was it *for*, then, after all—
that cosmic labor,
the lumbering stars, the planets,
earth, and voluptuous Eden—and yes,
His one big gamble: Adam, Eve,
the only things He couldn't be quite sure of.

And yet of course He *was* sure, had
fondled the whole thing in His lonely mind
since—well, forever—all
programmed there, ready
to play itself out just as He knew
it had to: the serpent, the fall,
the flaming sword, the steady slide into sin,
the flood . . .

So *why*, He asked Himself again,
what, after all, was the *point*? Just think
of all that bother—and now the obligation
of having to throw a fuss every time
He noticed a measly venial sin, some
small-time swindle—as if it made
a difference in the scheme of things.

Resting there, in that post-
partum depression—after all the planning,
the tough decisions, the perfect
execution—He knew
He knew the answer,
had to know it: He knew He was omniscient.
That's one of the things you know
When you're omniscient.
So had it been just the loneliness?
God knows (He thought) it's lonely at the top.
And yet . . .

Why, of course: it was the boredom,

the unbearable monotony
of endless time and empty space, and
angels—
everywhere He looked, a skyful of nothing
but angels and archangels, cherubim
and seraphim, rank upon rank, all
perfect. And virtuous. And dull.
Not even Satan and his little band
of hooligans had amused Him much,
the battle so pitifully short, so predictable,
the road to hell paved
with predestination. No,
if being God was going to be worth it all,
if He was going to get any fun
out of the job, He needed
something permanent, but evanescent,
something negligible, but outrageous.
He needed that big bang, of course,
and dying suns,
swirling gases, planets with protozoa,
worms, frogs, monkeys—but
He also needed
something—someone—special, someone
capable of understanding how cleverly
He'd stacked the deck—capable of knowing
how His omniscient
omnipotence smothered
justice, and mercy, and love—capable
of tragedy.
So at the last hour, on the last day,
He'd made up His mind: *do* it,
and call it Man, or Woman, or, why not,
create both of them, and let them
help each other
die.

He had to smile, remembering Satan,
down there now in that eternal fire.
Hell already existed, after all—so
let Man and Woman enter.

IV.

DARWIN 101

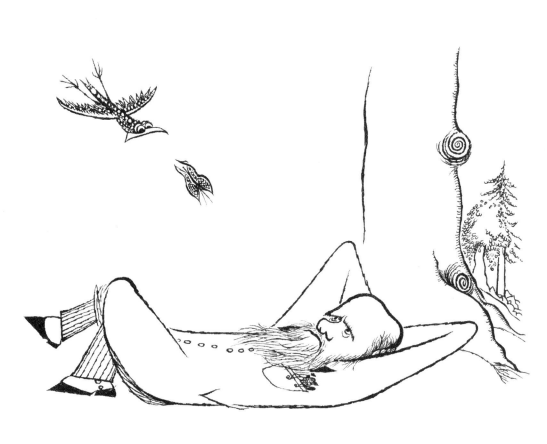

NOT FOR LOVE

"Contemplate a tangled bank . . . "
                    —Darwin, *The Origin of Species*

It is yes a green shimmer of beauty,
Of butterfly flashes of lemon,
The perfume of virginal roses,
And larks lifting lyrics to heaven . . .

And yes the larks love butterflies (for breakfast)
Raccoons love meadowlarks (at midnight dinners)
Roses hug their neighbors (till they wither)
Nature breeds good nature (in her winners).

So Brahmins love the beggars on the Ganges,
Bankers love their strip mines in Montana,
Pastors love their sheep, all ripe for fleecing,
And realtors love the trees in Indiana.

Moral:
Love suffers long and is kind of
Pathetically prone to be docile.
Darwin's advice to the prone is:
Beware of becoming a fossil.

WHY LAMARCK BECAME EXTINCT

"Acquisitions wrought by nature are preserved by reproduction."
—Lamarck, *Philosophie Zoologique*

Deep in the sleepy fields of August,
Who's making that chirr—cicadas or locusts?
And who's that, eating the buzzing bugs—
Mr. Toad or Mrs. Frog?
And who's the bird with the frog in his throat?
Is it a heron or is it a stork?

In this whirl of a world that so often confuses,
Here's a helpful fact:
Porpoises have rounded noses.
Dolphins have a beak.

That settles that, right off the bat,
But one more fact won't hurt us:
All tortoises are turtles, but
Not every turtle's a tortoise.

We're on the spot, Free Will or not:
We may think it bathetic,
But the shape we've got was not begot
By choice—it's all genetic.

Our torsos may not be immortal,
But wishing will never usurp us.
Moral: a dolphin can never turn turtle,
And you can't be a tortoise on porpoise.

HOROSCOPE

Back in college I had a girl friend, Sue,
who'd never heard of the Second Law
of Thermodynamics, and couldn't have cared less
that E = mc squared; and if you asked her
who Darwin was, Sue'd say
he's a theory, not a fact.

But there was this one Indisputably Scientific Thing
Sue saw so clearly: that the sun,
due to Electro-Magnetic Vibrations,
Dominates the Personality—give
or take some minor manipulations from the Moon,
which, as everyone knows, rules the emotions;
Mars and Venus, which govern speech and love;
et cetera, et cetera.

No use objecting that she
was dishing out a lot of pre-
historic goulash cooked up by the Chaldeans
(and if they're so smart, where are they now?)—
Sue wouldn't listen.
I should have dated that other girl,
the down-to-earth geology major,
and gone somewhere and hammered. But
Sue always seemed so happy. We were "Getting Along
So Well," she said, because our Signs were Compatible—
the stars and planets had got us matched up right,
like a cosmic computer date.

And yet, for all that solar certainty,
ours was a tragic story:
Sue said I was Aquarius and she was Virgo.
OK, fine—but exactly why we were "Getting Along
So Well" was always a bit obscure to me.
Still, Sue was sure of it—until
that unfavorable night when I refused to light
her thirteenth cigarette.
I kept telling her I wished she'd quit smoking,

partly because whenever I kissed her,
I could smell her lungs turning to tar,
and partly because I have this obsessive fear
that I'm going to die from secondhand smoke.
Sue'd only say, "Baby,
if that ciggy-boo's got your number on it,
it's got your number on it."

Well, this one star-crossed night I flatly refused
to light her up another filtered
death-wish. Instead, for three dramatic minutes,
I quoted from memory the cancer-mortality figures.
When I finished, having proved conclusively
that she had one foot stuck in an early grave,
she was fuming. "Buster!" she barked (that's not
my real name). "Just *when* did you say
your birthday was?"
"February, I told you."
"Yeah but *when* in February?"
"Nineteenth."
"Nine*teenth*? *When* on the nineteenth? *Where*?"
I told her. Quick as a Sagittarius, she grabbed
this little black book she always carries,
and for a tense sixty seconds, in the glow of her lighter,
there was not a sound in the county
but her sharp little "*Ooh's*" and "*My Gawd's!*"
When her head came up at last,
gaunt as a skull in the flickering flame,
something had altered the universe:
"*Sooo!*" she croaked, like an outraged crow,
"You claim to be an Aquarius—
when you were born after two P.M. in Noble County,
and Uranus was conjunct with Saturn, and square
to the progressed Mercury! And Venus was being *trined*
by the retrograding Mars! *And the Sun*," she screeched,
"the *Sun* was sextile to *Jupiter*, and semi-sextile
to the transiting *Neptune*! And the *Moon*
was nowhere *near* the seventh *house*!

And *you* claim to be an *Aquarius!*"
"B-b-but *I* never said—I mean
it was *you* who told *me* . . . " Sue wasn't
listening. "You *did*! Passed yourself off
as a vigorous, gregarious Aquarius—
when you're nothing but an *absentminded Pisces! Pretending*
to be generous and understanding, when all the time
you only lacked self-confidence—*just like a Pisces!*
Putting on like a humanitarian Aquarian, when, in fact,
you're just a sentimental Pisces who can't face reality!
Oh, now it all makes *sense! No wonder*
we weren't Getting Along! Hypocrite!
Take me home!"

I did. And that was the last I ever saw
of Sue. My roommate dated her later,
and other guys down the hall, and they all swore
Sue was the most voluptuous Virgo
they'd ever known.
Me, I married that geology major, a solid,
earthy girl, in hard times a real rock—
but I must admit, she has her own ways
of discovering my faults.

ET TU, GALILEO?

"The Eagle has landed."
—first man on the moon, 1969

"Maybe Darwin was right, after all."
—Pope John Paul II, 1996

Here in these devout Italian digs,
Hung with bleeding hearts and dying Jesus,
TV shows astronauts with little picks
Chipping chunks of greenish lunar cheeses.

The Vatican's abruptly overrun
With cardinals and bishops in collision—
The Pontiff pleads for prayer, but everyone
Is watching heresy on television.

Oh, Galileo, your retaliation
Is palpable as papal persecution:
Apollo shines your sunny vindication
On Copernicus, the Pill, and evolution.

By satellite, TV now tells the popes:
Look what comes of knocking telescopes.

PRAIRIE DOGS

"Prairie dog villages used to extend for hundreds of miles across the plains. One city contained more than 400 million of these ground squirrels. But 250 of them would eat as much as a cow, so prairie dogs were doomed."
—Desert Museum, Tucson, Arizona

"We must welcome more babies to the banquet of life."
—Pope Paul VI

Zoologists are all agog
At this imposter of a dog
Whose fierce fertility and brains
Civilized the western plains:
Taking to himself a wife,
He made a banquet out of life
And bred a swarm of boys and girls—
A great society of squirrels.

Life was simple, life was sport,
When one day everything ran short:
The five-year plan for grass was clouded,
Burrows all seemed overcrowded.
"Too many cows," they started to fuss,
"and what's more, there are too many of *us*."

Today, like aardvarks, yaks, and gnus,
Prairie dogs are kept in zoos.
Surviving rodents, may we hope
You have a message for the pope?

INTELLIGENT? DESIGN?

(To the tune of "Battle Hymn of the Republic")

Your eyes have seen a blurry scene
    That's only known to man:
Your optic nerves are backward and
    Have been since time began.
That's what the preachers tell you is
    God's very special plan:
    Intelligent Design!

Glory, Glory, Hallelujah!
Making-do will have to do ya.
Beware the swindlers who voodoo ya
With *Intelligent Design!*

You wish a guy's urethra did
    The jobs that were proposed:
Both lover's clout and waterspout
    Is what you had supposed.
Alas, the Great Designer squeezed
    A prostate 'round your hose:
    Intelligent Design!

    Glory, Glory, Hallelujah!
    Nowhere does the Bible clue ya
    That your glands would soon subdue ya:
    Intelligent Design!

Your breasts get lumps, your heart goes thump,
    Your hips are giving in.
Childbirth is a horror 'cause
    Your pelvis is too thin,
And osteoporosis is
    Your Maker's little whim:
    Intelligent Design!

    Glory, Glory, Hallelujah!
    The Great Designer knows what's due ya,
    Nothing else can stick it to ya
    Like *Intelligent Design!*

PHILIP APPLEMAN has published seven previous volumes of poetry, including *New and Selected Poems, 1956–1996* (University of Arkansas Press), as well as three novels, including *Apes and Angels* (Putnam), and five nonfiction books, including the widely used Norton Critical Edition of *Darwin*. His poetry has won many awards, including a fellowship from the National Endowment for the Arts, the Castagnola Award from the Poetry Society of America, the Friend of Darwin Award from the National Center for Science Education, and the Humanist Arts Award of the American Humanist Association. He has given readings of his poetry at the Library of Congress, the Guggenheim Museum, and many universities. He is Distinguished Professor Emeritus at Indiana University, a founding member of the Poets Advisory Committee of Poets House, New York, a former member of the governing board of the Poetry Society of America, and a member of the Academy of American Poets, PEN American Center, and Poets & Writers, Inc.

ARNOLD ROTH's cartoons and illustrations have appeared in *The New Yorker, Playboy, Punch, Esquire,* and many other publications. He is a member of the Society of Illustrators and past president of the National Cartoonists Society. His drawings and prints are in the collections of the Philadelphia Museum of Art, the International Museum of Cartoon Art, the Ohio State University, and other institutions and private collections. He has lectured widely, at the National Art Gallery, Princeton University, Yale University, Pratt Institute, the Parsons School, and other venues. Books he has written and illustrated include *Pick a Peck of Puzzles* (Norton), *A Comick Book of Sports* (Scribner's), and *No Pain, No Strain* (St. Martin's). He has previously illustrated books and book jackets by John Updike, George Plimpton, Bennett Cerf, and others.